CHAPTER 1

THE REAL ESTATE INVESTMENT ODYSSEY

This chapter serves as your compass, guiding you through the labyrinth of real estate investment rationale. Before diving into this realm, it's essential to cleanse your canvas of preconceived notions. Through these pages, you'll come to understand why real estate investment could be a symphony of opportunity for you, and why it might not fit snugly into your current life canvas.

Decoding the Enigma: Why Take the Real Estate Plunge?

Imagine the vast expanse of the US real estate market, valued at a staggering $33.6 trillion—a colossal realm of potential at your fingertips. Yet, remember that real estate is more than just an investment; it's a journey that necessitates aligning your financial stars, goals, and mindset. So, let's peel back the layers and explore why real estate investment can be your ultimate game-changer:

The Stream of Steady Cash Flow: Real estate's siren song lies in its ability to generate consistent cash flow. Your investment doesn't sit idle in a dormant account; it dances, yielding income. Cash flow is the rhythm of income versus expenses like mortgages and maintenance.

Positive cash flow means profits, negative indicates losses. Real estate's power to provide ongoing positive cash flow lays the foundation for future financial symphonies.

Tax Breaks and Benefits: Delve into the real estate treasure trove, and you'll unearth various tax advantages that can revolutionize your financial landscape. Think of the 1031 exchange, a magic wand for those reinvesting property sale proceeds. Then there are tax write-offs, a portfolio of deductions including maintenance, property taxes, and more. And don't forget depreciation deductions that can significantly reduce your tax burden.

The Elegance of Passive Income: Real estate offers the potential for passive income streams, where your investments clock in the hours for you. But, be patient—passive income doesn't manifest overnight. Whether it's astute property management or investment avenues like REITs, passive income emerges as a reward for those who play the long game.

Immunity Against Inflation's Sting: Inflation gnaws at your money's value over time. Consider this: in 1913, a dollar from then is equivalent to $26 now. Contrast that with the erosion of savings in bank accounts. Enter real estate—the appreciating phoenix that counters inflation's sting.
Real estate's value grows, and your investment gains momentum, a secure haven in the storm.

The Symphony of Diversification: In the grand orchestra of investment, real estate introduces harmony and stability. Amid market tumult, real estate maintains its melody, adding a unique rhythm to your investment portfolio. Diversification becomes your shield against market turbulence.

Essential Prerequisites for the Real Estate Overture

While real estate's stage beckons, it demands prerequisites for a stellar performance. Before you grace the spotlight, consider the following elements:

The Financial Prelude: Harmony in finances is essential—a symphony of savings, credit rating, and insurance coverage. Savings with an emergency fund cushion you against life's whims. A credit score is your ticket to favorable borrowing, and insurance creates a safety net.

Capital's Crescendo: Sufficient capital is the crescendo before the symphony begins. It's not about footing the entire bill, but meeting down payment requirements. Different lenders, different requirements—research is your tuning fork. Experts say, allocate 20% for a harmonious equity balance.

The Numerical Libretto: Real estate is a number's game; its symphony is composed of metrics like cash flow, mortgage payments, and returns.
Numerical fluency is your instrument—emotion takes a back seat, and prudent decisions take center stage.

The Sonata of Strategy: Real estate isn't about random notes—it's a symphony of strategy. Know the difference between jobs (flipping, wholesaling) and investing (holding). Craft a long-term strategy, where your assets crescendo into a harmonious symphony of wealth.

The Visionary Overture: An investor's vision is the overture to a symphony of success. See potential where others see mundane. Properties with hidden allure can transform with a touch. Extend your vision to market trends, neighborhoods, and enduring investment aspirations.

Is the Real Estate Sonata Right for You?

The prospect of real estate may resonate, but the stage requires preparation. Before the curtain rises, consider these factors:

The Financial Prelude: Without financial alignment, the symphony stumbles. Savings, credit rating, insurance—these are your prerequisites for a harmonious overture.

The Capital Crescendo: Capital readiness is paramount. Lenders demand a down payment—meet it for entry to the symphony.

The Numerical Libretto: Numerical fluency is the score to follow. A lack of number-savviness leads to dissonance in your investment symphony.

The Sonata of Strategy: Strategy orchestrates your journey. Without a roadmap, you'll find yourself lost in a cacophony of missteps.

The Visionary Overture: An investor's vision is your crescendo. Failure to perceive potential stifles your investment symphony's harmonious progression.

The Overture Concludes

The decision to traverse the real estate realm is yours. These chapters serve as your compass, directing you through the wilderness of real estate investment. The symphony of real estate's allure and its prerequisites must harmonize with your aspirations and circumstances. Armed with knowledge, you're poised to compose your own financial opus.

CHAPTER 2

PAVING THE PATH TO TRIUMPH
IN REAL ESTATE INVESTMENT

In the realm of investors, battles are first fought and won within the mind. An investor's greatest weapon is a steady temperament, relied upon especially during turbulent times. Optimism flourishes when all is well, but maintaining positivity amidst adversity is the true litmus test. When my own investment journey shifted from stocks to real estate due to losses, it presented a choice: surrender to lost dreams or seek alternative avenues. Investing, in any guise, shapes your resilience, and real estate is no exception. This chapter delves deep into crafting the indispensable mindset essential for navigating the labyrinthine world of real estate investment.

Transitioning from the insights of the previous chapter that outlined the stepping stones to success in real estate, we now delve further into fashioning an actionable approach. Finances, akin to personal fingerprints, assume varied forms for each individual. Despite the personal touch, a collective framework can be devised to enhance the prospects of success.

Before You Take the Plunge: Nuggets from Real Estate Investment

Perhaps towering property prices intimidate you, but innovative financing can substantially slash initial investments. Creative financing, the art of leveraging others' capital for profit, stands as a beacon in real estate investing. Mastering the nuances of creative financing can alter your financial trajectory.

Finding the Starting Line: Tales from the Trenches

Curiosity sparks—how does one embark on the journey of real estate investment? The narratives of individuals like Melanie Bajrovic offer a treasure trove of insights. Melanie, a 27-year-old bartender turned investor, provides a roadmap for novices. The perennial challenge of insufficient funds is surmounted with her approach—starting small, concentrating on single-family units, accumulating capital, and subsequently venturing into commercial properties. Melanie's odyssey from bartender to millionaire investor serves as a testament to the transformative potency of a meticulously plotted strategy.

Cracking the Mindset Code

What separates triumphant investors from the rest? It's not just sweat equity, available capital, or serendipity. The linchpin is the investing mindset. This mental paradigm molds responses to setbacks and dictates reactions during adversity. Let's dissect this mindset into two fundamental dimensions: attitudinal and financial.

Attitudinal Anchors

Behind the veneer of success lies a labyrinth of diligence and grit. Successful individuals cloak their relentless grind, often making the journey appear effortless. There are no shortcuts to the zenith, and any claim of effortless success merits scrutiny. Drawing from years as a real estate investor, I've gleaned that shortcuts are mirages. Here's how you can foster the attitudinal shifts vital for the right investing mindset:

> Embracing the Leap of Conviction: Real estate success springs from unwavering faith in your endeavor. Amid dissenting voices and perceived risks, steadfast adherence to calculated strategies mitigates risk. Understand that risk can never be eradicated entirely; prudent planning diminishes risk without nullifying it.

> Nurturing Networks: Prosperity in real estate hinges on collaborative alliances. Networking is your most prized possession. Authentic connections transcend the exchange of business cards; they involve reciprocal value and enduring relationships. Referrals, the lifeblood of networking, fortify bonds and yield enduring dividends.

> A Perpetual Learning Stance: Flourishing doesn't breed complacency; it thrives on perpetual learning. As markets flux, adaptability is paramount. A real estate investor's expertise spans beyond property—comprising legalities, maintenance, and more. Absorb the basics across diverse disciplines.

> Embracing Uncontrollable Variables: Not every element lies within your sphere of influence. A rigid stance against uncontrollable factors hampers progress. Acknowledging elements beyond control fosters strategic adaptation and amplifies resilience amidst tumultuous times.

> Mastering Visualization: Belief births reality. Visualization transmutes dreams into tangible existence. Engage your senses to vividly envisage your real estate aspirations. From vision boards to potent mental imagery, visualize your aspirations with crystalline precision.

Financial Foundations

The symphony of financial acumen harmonizes savings, credit stewardship, and insurance provisions.

A methodical approach underpins a robust financial underpinning for real estate investment. Address these dimensions through actionable strategies:

> The 50/30/20 Rule for Fiscal Alchemy: Dispel the notion that budgets restrict desires. The 50/30/20 rule offers an equilibrium, allocating 50% to necessities, 30% to desires, and 20% to savings. The envelope system amplifies this budgeting methodology.

> Taming Debt-to-Income Ratio: Financial equilibrium dwells in maintaining a debt-to-income ratio below 36%, with housing costs beneath 28%. Real estate investment necessitates acute comprehension of this ratio to ensure sustained fiscal well-being.

> Elevating Your Credit Rating: Elevate your credit score through a multifaceted strategy. Timely, consistent payments, judicious credit card usage, and prudent credit utilization contribute to an upward trajectory. Scrutinize your credit reports annually for inaccuracies.

> Comprehensive Shields: Safeguard your investments with comprehensive insurance coverage. Delve into options like liability insurance, hazard coverage, flood safeguards, tenant rent default insurance, and more. Collaborate with an insurance broker to tailor coverage to your unique imperatives.

The Essence of Mindset

As a contemporary real estate investor, you navigate a labyrinth of challenges. From embracing digital domains to unraveling funding intricacies, tenant stewardship, and income volatility, your mindset not only steers your course but molds your triumphs. Embrace the journey with an empowering mindset, for it serves as the compass unlocking your latent potential in the landscape of real estate investment.

CHAPTER 3

NAVIGATING THE BLUEPRINT FOR ACHIEVEMENT

The journey to cultivating the right mindset, as discussed in the previous chapter, is a gradual process. One doesn't acquire it overnight; rather, it evolves continuously through learning and influences your thinking in subtle yet impactful ways. With the foundational understanding of this mindset in place, you've taken your first stride towards prosperous investing. Now, let's proceed to the next phase: the art of devising strategic plans to propel your journey further. Just as you wouldn't board a train without a destination in mind, embarking on an investment without meticulous planning can lead to misdirection. Our aim is to explore the dimensions of converting your aspirations into thoughtfully orchestrated plans in this chapter, as we lay the groundwork before diving into concrete investment techniques.

Embracing the Crucial Role of Planning

The metamorphosis of your investment mindset is an ongoing voyage, shaped by continuous learning. With this crucial understanding at hand, it's time to elevate your trajectory with well-defined planning.

Just as a journey necessitates a map, successful investments require comprehensive plans. The absence of such plans is akin to wandering in a haze; it's easy to lose your way when the destination remains undefined. However, an effective plan doesn't merely provide a route, it accommodates the unexpected through spontaneity.

The Nexus of Goals and Strategic Blueprint

Transforming your investment dreams into actionable realities hinges on goal setting. Having assimilated the nuances of budgeting and financial dynamics, you're now poised to align your fiscal journey with your overarching vision. Financial prowess paves the path to opportunities, making goal setting a critical juncture.

Much like the significance of a clear vision in real estate, a corresponding financial vision is indispensable to steer your investment voyage. Consider where you envisage yourself five years down the line, the investments in sync with your aspirations, the allocation of funds, and the timeframes involved. These investment goals form the cornerstone on which your strategic plans will be constructed.

The SMART Approach to Goal Articulation

Effective goal setting demands precision and tangibility. The SMART framework — Specific, Measurable, Achievable, Relevant, and Time-bound — serves as the compass for this navigation:

Specific: Translate abstract aspirations into tangible, well-defined goals. Document your objectives with meticulous detail, painting a vivid picture in your mind.

Measurable: Goals without quantifiable metrics remain elusive. Attach measurable criteria to your objectives, enabling objective measurement of progress.

Achievable: While optimism is valued, attainability mitigates unrealistic expectations. Strive for realism, aligning goals with your existing resources and capacities.

Relevant: Personal resonance is pivotal for sustained commitment. Ensure your goals align with your values, reinforcing your dedication to their attainment.

Time-bound: Set temporal boundaries to infuse your goals with urgency. Determine clear deadlines for goal accomplishment, reducing ambiguity.

Embodied Vision within Business Blueprints

In the narrative of your investment odyssey, a business plan emerges as the compass, providing direction and coherence.

Beyond a mere schematic, a business plan encapsulates your investment ethos, predicting costs, clarifying operations, and charting strategies for goal fulfillment.

Key Pillars of a Comprehensive Business Plan

Well-Defined Goals: Reframe your SMART goals, integrating both short-term and long-term perspectives. Short-term objectives act as stepping stones toward broader aims.

Vision Statement: Your business's ethos forms your brand identity. Craft an evocative vision aligned with your values, shaping how your enterprise is perceived.

SWOT Analysis: Probe into Strengths, Weaknesses, Opportunities, and Threats. This introspective evaluation illuminates your competitive landscape, guiding strategic choices.

Business Strategy: Your chosen investment strategies anchor this section. Whether centered on wholesaling, flipping, or renting, these strategies direct your efforts.

Financial Report: This segment quantifies fiscal dimensions, encompassing operational costs, income projections, and profit and loss assessments.

Exit Strategies: Prudent planning mandates contingency solutions. Outline exit strategies to navigate adverse scenarios, bolstering resilience.

Executing the Blueprint: Crafting Your Business Plan

Your business plan surpasses mere words; it's a living script guiding your trajectory. Executing it effectively entails synchronizing the blueprint with your intent and audience:

Customized Introduction: Tailor your plan's introduction to resonate with your target audience — lenders, clients, or team members. Exude conviction in your expertise.

Case Studies for Clarity: Elaborate on your vision through case studies, distilling complex transactions for outsiders while showcasing your adeptness.

Adaptive Vision: Recognize your business's evolution. Regularly update your plan to reflect market shifts, fine-tuning your approach.

Assembling a Dream Team for Triumph

In real estate, solo endeavors yield limited results. Constructing a robust team augments your potential, transforming aspirations into achievements. Professionals across domains become your allies, enhancing your expertise and extending your reach.

A few indispensable members of your real estate dream team include:

Real Estate Agents: Cultivate relations with agents sharing your investment vision. Engage multiple agents for varied property leads.

Real Estate Attorney: Secure legal counsel for drafting documents and navigating potential legal challenges, safeguarding your investments.

Lenders: Foster lender relationships, collaborating to secure project financing. Trust and mutual benefit form the bedrock of these partnerships.

CPA: A Certified Public Accountant imparts fiscal guidance, steering your business toward wealth-building strategies and optimal tax solutions.

Property Manager: As investments grow, delegate operational tasks to property managers, freeing your focus for expansion.

Contractors and Handymen: Cultivate a network of skilled professionals to execute projects and maintain properties with precision.

Home Inspector: Count on inspectors to unearth hidden property flaws, mitigating investment risks.

Mortgage Broker: Tap into brokers' negotiation acumen for favorable lending terms and conditions.

Property Appraiser: Engage appraisers to ensure equitable valuations, guiding informed investment choices.

Accountability Partner: A confidant or mentor steers you right, offering impartial advice in challenging moments.

Cultivating Adaptability and Growth

In today's digital era, resources abound. As you embark on your real estate expedition, a wealth of information awaits exploration. Books, websites, and apps provide comprehensive insights, empowering informed decision-making. A few standout resources to commence your real estate voyage encompass:

Books:

"The Book on Rental Property Investing" by Brandon Turner
"How to Invest in Real Estate" by Joshua Dorkin and Brandon Turner
"The Millionaire Real Estate Investor" by Gary Keller
"What Every Real Estate Investor Needs to Know About Cash Flow" by Frank Gallinelli
"Crushing It in Apartments and Commercial Real Estate" by Brian Murray

Websites:

Roofstock Marketplace
Fortune Builders
BiggerPockets
Millionacres
For Sale By Owner (FSBO)

Apps:

Zillow
Rentometer
Deal Machine
Stessa
PayYourRent

Leverage these resources as instruments for perpetual growth and learning. Embrace technology to streamline your real estate journey, simplifying intricate tasks and broadening your horizons.

In Summation

Real estate triumph materializes through an intricate tapestry of factors, each weaving into the fabric of accomplishment. This chapter has illuminated the path towards translating aspirations into well-structured plans.

The subsequent chapter will delve into the practical techniques of real estate investment, grounding these concepts into actionable strategies. Your journey toward real estate prosperity gains momentum as you weave your unique narrative, blending knowledge, strategy, and execution into a symphony of achievement.

CHAPTER 4

EXPLORING THE ARRAY OF REAL ESTATE INVESTMENT STRATEGIES

When it comes to seeking financial guidance, it's not uncommon to encounter staunch advocates of a single investment strategy, touting it as the only path to prosperity. Stock enthusiasts may proclaim that investing in stocks is the ultimate key, while mutual fund proponents insist that safety lies in mutual funds. Even within the realm of real estate, you might come across enthusiasts who firmly believe that their preferred method is the sole route to success. However, this perspective is not only narrow but also misguided.

Consider this scenario: imagine you want to travel from New York to Delaware. Would it be accurate if someone told you that your only option is to take the train? Certainly not. While the train is a viable choice, it's not the only one. You could opt for a plane, a bus, or even choose to drive. In the same vein, the world of real estate investing offers a multitude of paths, each catering to different preferences and circumstances. The strategy you choose depends entirely on your unique needs and financial situation.

What I find particularly fascinating about real estate investing is the wealth of options it provides, each leading to a distinct destination. Whether you're looking to build a robust portfolio or secure steady rental income, real estate offers an array of strategies that align with your goals. You have the freedom to select the approach that resonates most with you, and even pivot to a new one when the time is right.

In this chapter, we embark on a journey through the diverse strategies available to real estate investors. While each of these strategies could warrant an entire book of its own, my aim here is to offer a comprehensive overview, allowing you to explore and delve deeper into those that resonate with you. From rental properties to house flipping, and from REITs to BRRRR investing, we'll examine the pros and cons of each, equipping you with valuable insights to shape your investment journey.

Reshaping Real Estate Investment Strategies

Strategy 1: Rental Properties (Buy-and-Hold Approach)

One enduring strategy is rental property investment, often referred to as the buy-and-hold approach.

What makes this strategy enticing is its ability to combine short-term cash flow with long-term appreciation. As a property owner, you benefit not only from regular rental income but also from the property's appreciation over time. While the aim is to eventually sell the property at a profit, the term "buy and forget" doesn't apply here; investors strategically plan their exit, sometimes leveraging the 1031 exchange to defer capital gains taxes.

When considering rental properties, two critical factors come into play: cash flow and appreciation. Cash flow, comprising income and expenses, forms the backbone of rental property investing. Determining an appropriate rent based on market conditions, location, and property features is crucial. Equally important is accounting for various expenses, such as insurance, taxes, maintenance, and vacancies, to accurately calculate cash flow.

Appreciation, on the other hand, relies on factors like location, demand, and development in the area. Recognizing these factors assists in gauging whether a property's value is likely to increase over time. By carefully analyzing both cash flow and appreciation potential, investors can identify rental properties that align with their wealth-building goals.

Strategy 2: House Flipping

House flipping, a dynamic investment strategy, involves purchasing distressed properties, renovating them, and swiftly selling for a profit. The success of house flipping hinges on securing properties at prices considerably lower than their after-repair value (ARV). Renovations play a pivotal role in enhancing a property's value, making meticulous planning and execution paramount.

Renovation efforts extend beyond cosmetic updates and encompass critical aspects like roofing, interior enhancements, and landscaping. The key is to add substantial value to the property while ensuring that costs remain below the 75% rule—expenses shouldn't surpass 75% of the property's ARV.

Strategy 3: BRRRR (Buy, Rehab, Rent, Refinance, Repeat)

An increasingly popular strategy is BRRRR, an acronym that captures the sequence of steps involved: Buy, Rehab, Rent, Refinance, and Repeat. BRRRR combines various investment techniques to optimize returns. The crux is to purchase distressed properties, renovate them, rent them out for steady income, refinance to release capital, and then replicate the process for further investments.

The strategy's strength lies in the ability to recycle capital, enabling investors to continually reinvest in new properties. It requires careful attention to property acquisition, renovation, and tenant selection, all contributing to the eventual success of the BRRRR approach.

Strategy 4: Real Estate Investment Groups (REIGs) and Real Estate Investment Trusts (REITs)

For those seeking a less hands-on approach, REIGs and REITs offer alternatives that minimize direct involvement in property management. REIGs allow investors to pool resources and collectively invest in properties, leveraging shared expertise. REITs, on the other hand, are publicly traded entities that manage portfolios of income-generating properties, providing investors with diversification and liquidity.

Navigating the Pros and Cons

Each strategy presents a unique blend of advantages and challenges, tailored to different investor preferences. Rental properties offer a balance between cash flow and appreciation, while house flipping promises rapid profits but demands careful planning.

BRRRR investing maximizes returns through capital recycling, while REIGs and REITs provide passive participation.

By thoughtfully weighing these factors, you can align your chosen strategy with your financial aspirations. Embracing the diversity of real estate investment approaches grants you the tools to navigate the intricate landscape confidently. Remember, your investment journey is uniquely yours, and the strategy you choose should mirror your objectives, risk tolerance, and vision for financial success.

CHAPTER 5

THE LANDSCAPE OF REAL ESTATE FINANCING STRATEGIES

The allure of easy loans often fades when one finds themselves on the borrowing end. The lending and borrowing process, whether for small or substantial sums, is often anything but straightforward. However, for real estate investors, embracing this process is essential, as loans are a fundamental tool for entering the market. Shifting from viewing loans as obstacles to seeing them as allies can transform your investment journey.

Loans are the cornerstone of real estate investment, allowing investors to leverage resources and make lucrative deals. As a seasoned real estate practitioner, I can attest that selecting the right lending approach and forging partnerships with the right lenders can make or break your investment ventures. In this chapter, we'll embark on a comprehensive exploration of the most prevalent methods investors use to secure financing in the dynamic world of real estate.

Our focus will encompass an array of financing strategies, ranging from the conventional to the unconventional.

While the realm of real estate financing is vast, we'll start by delving into the financing avenues that newcomers are most likely to encounter. The subsequent chapters will introduce more advanced and unique financing methods. Regardless of the approach, the goal remains constant: ensuring that a lack of funds never becomes a barrier to your success.

Navigating the Borrowing Odyssey

Before setting sights on properties, it's imperative to secure pre-approval for a loan. Distinct from pre-qualification, pre-approval entails a comprehensive assessment of your credit history, income, and valuable assets. This assessment culminates in determining the debt-to-income (DTI) and loan-to-value (LTV) ratios, crucial benchmarks for loan eligibility. Pre-approval, however, has a limited validity period—typically around three months—requiring property selection within this timeframe.

With a property identified and a Purchase and Sale agreement signed, the lender's role resurfaces. The loan application undergoes underwriting, scrutinizing property documents and agreements.

This process is followed by property appraisal and a subsequent round of underwriting, culminating in loan approval. Although intricate, this multi-step process ensures thorough due diligence in securing suitable financing.

Exploring Conventional Home Loans

Conventional home loans, often synonymous with mortgages, offer a range of options to borrowers. Fixed-rate mortgages lock in an initial interest rate for the entire loan tenure, providing stability for profitability analysis. Adjustable-rate mortgages (ARMs) begin with a fixed rate before transitioning to a variable rate. Interest-only loans, a deceptive option, require interest payments initially, with principal repayment deferred. Choosing the right loan duration is also paramount, as shorter loans entail lower interest payments over time.

Delving into Conforming Loans

Backed by agencies like Fannie Mae, Freddie Mac, and Ginnie Mae, conforming loans adhere to standardized guidelines. FHA loans cater to low to moderate income families, while VA loans offer military personnel and their spouses low-interest rates with no down payment.

USDA loans target low-income rural buyers, offering minimal interest rates and down payment requirements. The backing of these agencies translates into favorable interest rates for conforming loans.

Navigating Hard Money Loans

Unlike traditional loans, hard money loans prioritize collateral over creditworthiness. Backed by the property's value, these short-term bridge loans cater to house flippers and BRRRR investors. Their hallmark is quick closing times and flexible terms, although the high interest rates necessitate swift repayment.

Exploring Private Money Loans

Private money loans operate informally, often facilitated by friends, family, or investors. Terms vary depending on the lender, necessitating careful consideration to avoid predatory lending practices. While such loans offer flexibility, maintaining a business-like approach is vital to preserving personal relationships.

Leveraging Home Equity

Home equity serves as a valuable financing channel for investors.

Home equity lines of credit (HELOCs) and home equity loans allow borrowers to tap into their equity. HELOCs function like credit cards, enabling borrowing within a predetermined limit over a set period. Home equity loans provide borrowers with a lump sum against their equity, offering funds for diverse expenses.

Selecting the right financing avenue requires a comprehensive evaluation of your investment objectives, risk tolerance, and available resources. The diverse array of strategies, from conventional loans to private lending, presents distinct advantages and disadvantages. Tailoring your approach to align with your unique investment goals ensures a smooth path to success. As we conclude our exploration of these common financing routes, we'll venture into lesser-known methods in the upcoming chapters, broadening your financing horizons even further.

CHAPTER 6

FINANCIAL POTENTIAL WITH PERSONAL AND BUSINESS LOANS

In the realm of real estate, having access to financial resources can often be the bridge that leads to triumph. While it's clear that money alone can't purchase happiness, it does offer a sense of security and a gateway to a world of possibilities. For real estate investors, comprehending the intricacies of financial pathways is as vital as recognizing promising deals. This chapter delves into the two distinct avenues of personal and business loans, offering insights into their unique roles in your real estate journey.

The Distinctive Lure of Personal and Business Loans

You might question why we've chosen to spotlight personal and business loans separately, given that both involve borrowing. The reasoning behind this distinction is two-fold. First, many investors tend to overlook personal and business loans due to a lack of familiarity. Second, these loan categories diverge from the traditional collateral-based model, a deviation that warrants thorough examination.

This chapter seeks to shed light on the untapped potential of personal and business loans. By comprehending their particular advantages and nuances, you'll be equipped to wield them effectively as tools for real estate prosperity.

Charting New Paths with Loans: Kendra Barnes' Journey

Kendra Barnes' journey through real estate investing is a testament to the transformative power of unconventional approaches. Kendra stumbled upon real estate investing while playing a board game named Cashflow—an unlikely origin. Previously an economist in the US government, real estate wasn't on her radar until fate intervened. Facing financial constraints with a family to support, Kendra and her husband chose a distinctive route. They secured a loan from their retirement funds to initiate their real estate journey. This unorthodox strategy allowed them to acquire their first rental property, setting in motion a trajectory that eventually led Kendra to transition from her desk job to becoming a full-time real estate investor.

Diverse Avenues of Personal Loans

Unlike loans earmarked for specific purposes, personal loans offer borrowers versatility in allocating funds.

These loans are not confined to designated uses like mortgages or car loans; instead, they can be used for various personal expenses. Personal loans adhere to standard loan features—interest rates, repayment periods, and monthly payments. Longer loan terms correlate with higher accumulated interest, much like the principles governing mortgages.

Personal loans can either be secured with collateral—retirement funds, vehicles—or unsecured, requiring no collateral. Unsecured personal loans tend to carry higher interest rates due to the perceived risk for lenders. Additionally, some lenders impose origination fees. Hence, meticulous comparison of terms and conditions across lenders is essential.

Nurturing Investments through Personal Loans

Utilizing personal loans for real estate investments demands thoughtful consideration. It's prudent to assess two scenarios where personal loans might be a strategic choice:

> Investments with Minimal Risk: Evaluating risk tolerance is paramount. Personal loans align well with low-risk investments, especially in areas with robust rental demand.
> Solid Credit Score Advantage: A strong credit score translates to favorable loan terms, enhancing investment potential. Borrowers with excellent credit scores can secure competitive interest rates, elevating profitability.

However, deploying personal loans for investments involves potential pitfalls:

> Underwater Investment Risks: Investments inherently carry uncertainty. If an investment underperforms, borrowers might incur more interest expenses than the asset's value.
> High Interest Rate Impact: Elevated interest rates can erode profits, particularly if returns fall short of the interest rate.
> Credit Consequences: Defaulting on personal loans can damage credit scores, impacting future borrowing prospects.

Thorough evaluation of both benefits and risks is imperative when considering personal loans for real estate investments.

Business Loans: Fostering Real Estate Growth

Adopting a business-centric perspective in real estate investing introduces a wealth of financing options, including business loans. Secured by business assets, these loans provide essential resources for property acquisition, development, and operations. Business loans offer a critical advantage by mitigating personal liability, a pivotal concern for investors exposed to potential risks.

Various real estate entities can harness the potential of business loans, such as sole proprietorships, limited partnerships (LPs), and limited liability companies (LLCs). Among these, LLCs stand out for their capacity to shield personal assets, optimize taxation, and establish a clear separation between personal and business finances.

The Art of Crafting an LLC

Forming an LLC is a pivotal step for investors seeking to establish a formal business structure. The process involves several key steps:

> Selecting a Fitting Name: Choose a name compliant with state laws and reflective of the business's LLC status.

> Designating a Registered Agent: Appoint a registered agent responsible for receiving legal communications on behalf of the LLC.

> Submitting Articles of Organization: Complete the necessary form detailing the LLC's purpose, management plan, registered agent information, and other relevant details.

> Crafting an Operating Agreement: Outline roles, responsibilities, profit distribution, and departure protocols within the LLC. Even single-member LLCs benefit from this document.

> Ensuring Compliance: Fulfill annual reporting obligations, pay fees, and acquire permits and licenses as required by state and federal regulations.

Navigating Business Loans for Diverse Entities

Business loans deliver an array of benefits compared to personal loans, particularly for LLCs.

With LLCs, personal liability is substantially reduced, ensuring a clear demarcation between personal and business assets.

Business loans offer higher borrowing limits, competitive interest rates, and extended repayment periods, facilitating substantial investment capital.

For enterprises, specialized options like blanket mortgages and portfolio loans provide distinct advantages.

Blanket mortgages consolidate multiple properties, streamlining management. Portfolio loans transcend conforming loan restrictions, offering greater flexibility and customization.

Conclusion

Thriving in real estate investing demands a multifaceted approach to financing. Personal and business loans provide unique avenues to capitalize on opportunities, enhance flexibility, and safeguard investments.

By navigating the nuances of personal loans and harnessing the power of business loans, you can strategically bolster your real estate portfolio and pave the way for enduring prosperity.

As you tread this path, remember that every financial decision must be grounded in a profound understanding of your distinctive investment goals, risk appetite, and long-term vision.

CHAPTER 7

THE POWER OF GOVERNMENT GRANTS

Igniting Investment Opportunities Through Grants

Diverse funding avenues exist in the realm of real estate investment, each with its unique appeal. Among them, grants stand out as a distinctive option that can provide financial backing without the weight of loans. Grants offer a window for investors with limited resources to grasp potentially lucrative opportunities without the burden of debt. Acknowledging their potential to reshape individual trajectories and invigorate economic landscapes, the US government actively employs grants to foster real estate investments. This chapter delves deep into the realm of government grants, unraveling the ways they empower investors to cultivate and expand their investment portfolios.

Deciphering the Essence of Grants

At first glance, grants represent a lifeline extended to eligible individuals or businesses, granting them funds without the requirement of repayment. It's crucial to dispel the notion that grants are a form of "easy money"; rather, they serve as targeted financial catalysts. Governments utilize grants strategically to advance specific community goals, energize economic progress, and bolster the housing market.

The crux of the matter is that grants aren't just about financial aid; they're about driving upward mobility, elevating living standards, and spurring economic vitality. Governments recognize the pivotal role of real estate in these pursuits, prompting them to offer grants as incentives for investment, thereby fostering a dynamic and resilient housing sector.

Classifying the Tapestry of Grants

The landscape of government grants is intricate, punctuated by diverse classifications based on funding origins and recipients. To simplify this complexity, let's zero in on four fundamental categories of grants that savvy real estate investors ought to comprehend:

Competitive Grants: These grants are subject to a selection process, where candidates are evaluated against specific criteria. Authorities then choose recipients based on the alignment between candidates and criteria.

Pass-through Grants: These grants channel federal funds through state or local governments to eligible recipients. They facilitate the dissemination of funds while leveraging existing administrative structures.

Formula Grants: Imposing predetermined standards, formula grants are non-competitive. All applicants fulfilling the criteria receive grants, though the monetary allocation may vary.

Continuation Grants: Characterized by renewable cycles, continuation grants may renew annually or at defined intervals. Grant renewal hinges on demonstrated outcomes, adherence to reporting guidelines, consistent communication, and a positive relationship with funders.

Investors must grasp these classifications in relation to their property types, whether public, private, or collective. Such understanding aids in pinpointing relevant grant opportunities aligned with their investment goals.

Charting the Course for Acquiring Grants

Securing an apt grant necessitates a systematic approach encompassing three critical facets:

Research: Commence with thorough research, the bedrock of grant acquisition. Start by engaging local Department of Housing and Urban Development offices, accessing insights into available grants. Government platforms such as hud.gov and grants.gov offer a wealth of information. Establishing relationships with officials facilitates navigation through the process.

Application: Crafting a compelling grant proposal, often referred to as grant writing, is pivotal. A well-structured proposal should encompass essential components like a succinct cover letter, an executive summary, a problem statement, defined objectives, strategies for business sustainability, and a transparent projected budget. Tailoring the proposal to resonate with the grant's objectives enhances its appeal to reviewers.

Follow-up: Maintaining consistent follow-up establishes an enduring presence in grant officials' minds, enhancing the prospect of consideration for future opportunities. Establishing rapport with grant officials can lead to proactive notifications about suitable grants.

Showcasing Noteworthy Government Grants for Real Estate Investors

While the landscape is rife with diverse government grants, the spotlight falls on five standout options for investors poised to harness grants for real estate ventures:

RESTORE Act Direct Component—Construction and Real Property Activities: Targeting the Gulf Coast region, this grant channels support into property development across Texas, Louisiana, Mississippi, Alabama, and Florida. Applicants must adhere to specified criteria and submit multiyear plans outlining their objectives.

HOME Investment Partnerships Program: With an annual allocation nearing $2 billion, this initiative prioritizes affordable housing for low-income segments. Funds are channeled through state and local governments, offering individual investors a collaboration route with eligible organizations.

Emergency Capital Repair Grant: This grant, facilitated by HUD, extends to multifamily rental property owners for urgent structural repairs and equipment replacement. The grant ceiling stands at $500,000.

Real Property Investment Grant: Investors can access up to $100,000 per qualifying property, with an overall cap of $5 million.

Neighborhood Stabilization Program (NSP) Grant: Tailored for neighborhoods grappling with multiple foreclosures, this grant facilitates acquiring properties below market value.

Navigating the Pros and Cons of Grant Utilization

Engaging with grants introduces a dual-edged dynamic that demands strategic navigation. While grants offer a non-repayable lifeline, they often entail commitments such as residence in the property for a defined period. This underscores the importance of building equity to ensure a seamless exit. Grants can also amplify an investor's reputation, positioning them favorably for additional grant opportunities.

Conversely, grants can impose restrictions on property choices and objectives, limiting the investor's autonomy in shaping their real estate endeavors.

Conclusion

Government grants illuminate an avenue rich with potential for real estate investors seeking alternatives to conventional loans. The diverse grant categories cater to varying property types and investment stages, offering a conduit for investors to amplify their portfolios, stimulate economic dynamism, and align their real estate ventures with broader community objectives. As you navigate this landscape, remember that meticulous research, strategic proposal crafting, and persistent follow-up are the compass points that guide you towards maximizing the benefits of grants and realizing your real estate investment aspirations.

CHAPTER 8

CROWDFUNDING FOR REAL ESTATE VENTURES

Visualize this scenario: You've meticulously crafted a real estate venture that holds immense promise. Countless hours have been invested in research, number crunching, and strategic planning. Yet, the project's scale places it beyond your financial grasp. Undeterred, you set out to present your proposition to affluent investors who could inject the necessary capital in return for substantial returns. But here's the twist – pitching your concept turns out to be more intricate than all your preparatory work combined. The outcome now hinges on their response, leaving you at the mercy of uncertainty.

Until a few years ago, this was the standard narrative for sourcing funds for ambitious real estate undertakings. Significant real estate ventures were typically the playground of the affluent, as their financial capacity allowed them to make substantial contributions. The general populace could only observe as these monumental projects unfolded. The status quo, however, has undergone a revolutionary shift, propelled by an innovative strategy known as crowdfunding.

In the ensuing chapter, we embark on an exploration of the intricacies of crowdfunding—an avant-garde approach to acquiring capital for your aspirational real estate aspirations.

Crowdfunding's Ascension: An Insight

The global crowdfunding market boasted a valuation of $151.9 billion in 2021, with projections indicating a staggering ascent to $1351.1 billion by 2030 (Report Ocean, 2023). This growth trajectory transcends mere expansion; it signifies a seismic transformation. The pivotal query: are you poised to evolve in tandem with this dynamic landscape?

Narratives of Transformation: An Exemplar

Dan's foray into real estate dates back to 2003, employing traditional routes. His passion for real estate kindled the creation of a system designed to generate passive income. While content within the contours of conventional methodologies, he's quick to recognize the transformative potential of online crowdfunding.

Dan's maiden crowdfunded real estate investment in 2016 unlocked avenues to approximately $100,000 in annual passive income from crowdfunded endeavors and an estimated $380,000 in total annual passive income from his comprehensive real estate portfolio. A life replete with cherished family moments, leisurely pursuits, and guiding novice investors elucidates the potency of crowdfunding.

A Paradigm Redefined: Crowdfunding Unveiled

The paradigm shift from conventional funding mechanisms was instigated by the JOBS Act of 2012, dispelling limitations on soliciting capital for real estate ventures. Developers could now openly canvass for funds online, transcending the confines of a restricted investor circle. However, this shift entails a multifaceted process that extends beyond mere advertising.

Crowdfunding platforms deviate from the norm of conventional real estate listings. Instead of showcasing properties directly, these platforms enable investors to secure stakes in entities undertaking real estate enterprises. As a sponsor seeking capital, you establish an autonomous entity entrusted with project execution and subsequently register it on a crowdfunding platform.

These platforms, subject to stringent regulation, undergo exhaustive scrutiny before endorsing project promotion.

Roles Defined: Architects and Patrons

The ecosystem of crowdfunding revolves around two pivotal archetypes—the sponsor and the investor. A comprehensive grasp of their respective roles is pivotal:

> Sponsor: Often synonymous with developers or facilitators, sponsors are entrusted with procuring capital for specific projects. Their mandate mirrors that of a traditional property procurer, encompassing deal origination, due diligence, negotiation, contractual formalities, and more. Sponsors orchestrate meticulous project blueprints and engage investors to finance their initiatives.
> Investor: Investors furnish the capital, facilitating projects without direct engagement in execution. Their function assumes a supervisory mantle, scrutinizing sponsor activities to ascertain project alignment with forecasted financial and perceptual tenets.

Assorted Investor Profiles

Investors span diverse categories contingent on their credentials:

Accredited Investors: Formal acknowledgment by the SEC earmarks accredited investors, necessitating compliance with specific criteria. This mandates a net worth exceeding $1 million, exclusive of primary residence, coupled with individual annual income surpassing $200,000 or combined income exceeding $300,000. Accredited investors boast SEC-recognized qualifications, designations, and experience.

Sophisticated Investors: Resonating with accredited investors, this faction lacks SEC accreditation while boasting substantive acumen, experience, and expertise.

Non-accredited Investors: Forming a substantial segment of the crowdfunding landscape, these investors lack SEC recognition or profound investment acumen.

The Yin and Yang of Crowdfunding: Pros and Cons

Crowdfunding's meteoric rise is substantiated by its inherent merits; however, it carries inherent caveats that warrant circumspection.

Advantages:

Streamlined Efficiency: Online accessibility streamlines investor outreach, facilitated via webinars and interactive platforms.

Robust Business Framework: Capital is secured without depleting personal credit, establishing venture-specific financing channels.

Dynamic Interaction: Crowdfunding nurtures transparent sponsor-investor dialogues, fostering iterative feedback loops for refinement.

Brand Amplification: Online campaigns fortify brand credibility, appealing to investors seeking adaptable, high-yield prospects.

Drawbacks:

Investor Surrender: Investors cede control in crowdfunding projects, potentially deterring those seeking an active role.

Protracted Commitment: Project timelines extending over years may discourage investors eyeing rapid returns.

SEC Constraints: SEC regulations constrain non-accredited investors' investment capacity, mandating sponsors to cultivate a broader investor base.

Epilogue: Deciphering Crowdfunding's Code

Crowdfunding emerges as a transformative channel for financing real estate enterprises, democratizing capital access. The dynamic interplay between sponsors and investors begets a symbiotic relationship, ensuring project actualization and oversight. Proficiency in the subtleties of crowdfunding empowers sponsors to tap into an expanding market, morphing visionary dreams into tangible reality. Simultaneously, it furnishes investors diverse entry points into the realm of real estate opportunities, fostering a win-win proposition for all stakeholders.
Angel investors may be found beyond the realm of well-known personalities; friends and family can also serve as potential sources of angel funds.

However, if these immediate connections are inadequate, a broader search is warranted. Critical attributes to seek in angel investors encompass:

Experience and Expertise: Angel investors contribute more than mere capital; their wisdom and experience can significantly enhance your entrepreneurial journey.

Ensuring their familiarity with your market and industry is pivotal, as this informs their potential contributions.

Calculated Risk-Taking: While angels are predisposed to embrace calculated risk, a balanced approach is vital. Evaluating their past investment choices offers insight into their risk appetite.

Realism and Pragmatism: Real estate inherently involves a longer-term perspective, necessitating an investor who aligns with your business vision. A convergence of expectations is critical.

Mentoring: An investor willing to offer guidance and insights can be immensely valuable. Early clarification regarding their anticipated level of involvement is essential.

Financial Stability: An investor's financial robustness is not to be underestimated, as it impacts their investment horizon and expectations regarding returns.

Trust and Connection: Above all, fostering mutual trust forms the bedrock of a successful collaboration. Establishing a solid relationship underpins the efficacy of your partnership.

Strategies for Identifying Angel Investors
Local Networking: Engaging with local investors can yield rapid traction, particularly when investors seek to witness the growth of businesses within their community.

Collegiate Connections: Many educational institutions host angel investor networks aimed at supporting initiatives launched by recent graduates.

Online Platforms: Leverage platforms such as AngelList, Angel Capital Association, Angel Forum, Gust, and Angel Investment Network to tap into a diverse pool of potential investors.

Key Insights for Presenting to Angel Investors

Effective pitching is an art that resonates with angel investors:

Grit and Tenacity: Passion and unwavering commitment are infectious. Demonstrate your emotional, financial, and physical investment in your entrepreneurial venture.

Crystal Clear Business Acumen: Profound knowledge of your market, competitors, and prevailing trends is indispensable. Investors rely on your expertise to drive returns.

Mastery of Financial Metrics: Proficiency in financial metrics—such as cash flow, property valuations, projected revenue, and budgeting—establishes your credibility.

Openness to Constructive Feedback: Investors value entrepreneurs receptive to input. Striking a balance between conviction and adaptability, based on evidence, is key.

Authentic Connection: While professionalism is important, authenticity resonates more deeply. Tailoring your pitch to align with investor expectations fosters trustworthiness.

Pros and Cons of Angel Investment

Pros:

Access to Capital: Angel investors are inclined to invest in promising opportunities.
Expertise and Networks: They bring valuable expertise, connections, and additional resources to the table.
Enhanced Credibility: Angel investment bolsters your venture's credibility.
Local Anchoring: Local investors often offer direct engagement and support.

Cons:

Equity Dilution: More investors translate to reduced ownership and decision-making authority.
Investor Expectations: High returns come with heightened performance expectations.
Limited Capitalization: Angel investment is frequently capped at smaller amounts.
Choice Limitations: Limited options might lead to pressured decisions due to

funding urgencies.

Conclusion: Angel Investors as Guiding Forces

Angel investors furnish not only financial backing but also mentorship and strategic networks. Navigating the angel investor landscape entails harmonizing expectations and forging a symbiotic relationship.

Leveraging local networks, online platforms, and strategic networking can guide you toward the ideal investor match. Delivering a compelling pitch, infused with authenticity, clarity, and numerical acumen, is paramount to securing their partnership. The journey with angel investors demands a delicate equilibrium between unwavering conviction and open receptiveness, ultimately steering you toward prosperity within the real estate arena.

Special Offer!

Loved Our Book? We're Excited To Give Back To Our Loyal Fans!

Get 5 Exclusive Digital Books For Free.

Email: infobookpub@Gmail.Com With The Subject As "Free Books"